I RHYME EVERY TIME

Where Poetry Meets Soul

Lisa Nicole W.

First Edition

ISBN: 979-8-9994657-0-2

Cover design by MosLeVaCha Distribution

Published by MosLeVaCha Distribution

Disclaimer: Selected poems in this collection may reflect lyrical inspiration from copyrighted songs. Any referenced material has been paraphrased and altered by the author. No copyrighted lyrics have been used verbatim.

Printed in the United States of America

Acknowledgments

I thank God for the gift of poetry and the courage to share it. To my son Lamauree, as a single mom, your presence gives me strength and keeps me moving forward. To my mother Rosetta, for all that you do, and to my sister Tawanna, for your guidance – thank you. To my family, friends, and all who spoke life into this dream – I am forever grateful. And to you, the reader, thank you for turning these pages; may you discover something here that truly speaks to you.

Love,
- Lisa

The Inspiration Behind the Book

Poetry has always been my safe space – a way to release what I felt when I didn't have the words to say it out loud. Over the years, it's helped me heal, express myself, and stay connected to who I truly am.

This book is more than just poems – it's a reflection of my journey. The ups, the downs, the lessons, the faith, the music, and the love that carried me through.

The titles pay tribute to songs and artists who inspired me – however, the stories behind each piece are uniquely mine.

Some poems will make you laugh, some will make you pause and reflect, and some may feel like they are telling your story too.

My hope is that these words inspire you, bring you comfort, or simply remind you that you are not alone.

Table of Contents

Hardships, Healing & Strength............. 26

Positivity, Growth & Motivation 35

Music, Rhythm & Artistic Inspiration...50

Self-Reflection & Life Lessons 59

WHERE I BEGIN

Our experiences shape us, but understanding our roots keeps us grounded. These poems explore my identity, beliefs, and the journey that defines who I am.

"Lisa Is My Name"

How's everyone doing? My name is Lisa!
From New Brunswick, New Jersey, off exit Nine,
Humble and cool, I stay nice and in line.

When it comes to looks, I'm not the worst or the best,
But I'm cute enough, with a smile that's blessed.
Not an army, but people can still salute,
With faith and drive, never staying mute.

Nobody's perfect, but I'm working to pass the test,
I'm all about growing, settling for more, not less.
My personality's solid, my profile on point,
Like Lloyd Banks, I give reasons to anoint.

At 5'3, my heart and soul are secure,
Don't let age fool you – I'm wise and mature.
Why let negativity ruin my day,
When opinions won't hold any sway.

No, I keep rising, staying uplifted,
Focused on growth, my path is gifted.
I know my worth, and in quality, I believe,
Willing to learn – that's the life I perceive.

Everything God provides is always a blessing,
Through highs and lows, we're all taught a lesson.
My poetry's real, it makes people think,
Some get speechless, amazed to the brink.

Life has its joys, but it's not a game,
So nice to meet y'all – **Lisa is my name.**

A Gift from God

"God Is Beyond Good"

God is good, all the time,
He blessed my soul with words that rhyme.
A gift so strong, a voice so clear,
Through every poem, I feel Him near.

I won't let struggles hold me back,
His guidance always keeps me on track.
Even when roads feel tough to climb,
His love uplifts me, time after time.

My talent's rare – it shines, it grows,
A gift from God, and that He knows.
Each verse I write, each line I share,
Is proof His presence is always there.

Hard work and faith can make you a star,
But walking with God will take you far.
His blessings flow, His love stands true,
Every poem I craft is a praise to You.

Never forget the grace He's shown,
Through Him, my words have truly grown.
Beyond the stars, where grace has stood,
No doubt at all – **God is beyond good!**

Inspired by Teddy Pendergrass

"My Greatest Inspiration"

There's so much in life that inspires me,
Great people noticed things I couldn't see.
Harold Melvin, the Blue Notes, and Teddy Pendergrass,
Legends of music, with style and class.

"My Greatest Inspiration" is a powerful, positive song,
Created just right, so smooth, not one part of it is wrong.
Not a single note feels out of place,
A melody crafted with elegance and grace.

Though many things inspire me, music leads the way,
Its essence uplifts me every single day.
Like warm encouragement from coast to coast,
Music is what I treasure the most.

I'm real glad that talent does not have an expiration,
Strength and Success is **my greatest inspiration.**

Self-Worth & Empowerment

These are my reminders to stay confident, know my worth, and never settle. It's about walking in your power – unapologetically.

Inspired by Morris Day and The Time

"Cool"

What's good, people? What's everyone up to?
As for me, I'm just living life, doing what I gotta do.
Each day brings change, yet my routine stays intact,
I move with style and faith – that's a fact.

I'm speaking of myself, not trying to brag,
My passion runs deep, it's more than swag.
Who else lives a lifestyle so fresh and in fashion,
Driven by purpose, fueled by passion.

Straight like that, no time to delay,
We need more smiles and fun every day.
It's never too late to spread joy and cheer,
Before, now, and later – all times are clear.

Take a moment to reflect, let memories shine bright,
Even school days that once brought you delight.
No matter what, I'll stick to my rule,
This sweet little lady is definitely **cool.**

Inspired by 702

"Steelo"

I love a person's Steelo just like 702,
It's great to have so much in common with you.
Kameelah, LaMisha, and Irish – voices shine bright,
Though looks catch the eye, personality feels more right.

Having style that's unique is a feeling I know,
And building a profile that reflects how I grow.
Irish Grinstead was a favorite, her spirit so rare,
Rest in peace to her, soaring with wings through the air.

I won't be a fool for anyone who thinks it's fine,
To compromise my values or cross the line.
With optimism, I'm waiting for Mr. Right to appear,
Hoping he shares his Steelo, making his intentions clear.

With every step of grace, you make your presence glow,
True connections blossom through your genuine **Steelo.**

Inspired by Joe Thomas

"Good Girl"

No doubt about it, I shine with a natural flow,
Writing poems with passion is how I let it show.
Joe once sang about good girls being gone every time,
But here I stand, with rhythm and rhyme.

Through challenges I face, I stand tall and strong,
With grace and resilience, I find where I belong.
Each step I take is guided by my light,
A journey of growth that feels just right.

A woman with style, heart, and a caring embrace,
Respectful and worthy, holding my place.
A bright smile that warms both day and night,
With every reason to be treated right.

Smart, sweet, with curls that twirl,
Always and forever, I'm a **good girl.**

Inspired by Billy Ocean

"Queen"

In a deck of cards, there's both queen and king,
Numbers and spades make it a special thing.
Queen Latifah's a legend, one of the best,
Her songs and her style stand out from the rest.

Billy Ocean's "Caribbean Queen" is pure delight,
A classic tune that still feels right.
Every woman is a queen, fierce and free,
A symbol of strength for the world to see.

Queens inspire greatness in all that we do,
With hearts of gold and visions that stay true.
Styles and fashion an endless array,
Worn with pride every single day.

A crown isn't needed to show your esteem,
For every woman shines bright as a **queen.**

Inspired by Keri Hilson

"Ladies, We Rock"

There are many good men in the world, that's true,
But ladies, we rock – it's more than a few.
Don't believe anyone who says we're not strong,
Both men and women shine, together we belong.

It's not just looks or talents on display,
It's the kindness and actions we show every day.
I've connected with people, building bonds so real,
It's a fact – these connections are part of the deal.

So many beautiful women in the world,
Short hair, long hair, straight, or curled.
Cool, loving, loyal, with charm so rare,
That's who I strive to be, beyond compare.

It feels good to succeed, to be proud and bold,
To embrace our strength and let self-worth unfold.
Confidence grows, it shines, it's true,
Ladies, we rise in all that we do.

The love for our gifts fills us with delight,
Amazing and powerful, it feels so right.
So, keep shining bright, keep breaking the lock,
Ladies, stand tall – because **ladies, we rock.**

Inspired by CeCe Peniston

"Keep On Walking"

Just keep on walking if you want to go,
That's the mindset some have when hearing the word, no.
CeCe Peniston's song from 1992 is a classic hit,
Full of empowerment and confidence, forever lit.

Life's too short for drama or vibes that aren't right,
Focus on what uplifts, let go of the fight.
CeCe boldly declared she was done with him for good,
And her words resonate – they're well understood.

While control isn't always in reach, voices must never fade,
Expression should shine with passion that won't degrade.
If someone steps away and decides to leave, let it be,
Resilience leads the way, remain strong and free.

This is a reminder to stand tall, no matter who's talking,
Let them choose their path, and just **keep on walking.**

Inspired by Big Daddy Kane

"Steppin"

If you think to half step, better think twice,
Do it all the way, let your purpose feel right.
Make it easy on yourself and those you meet,
Brighten the day and keep life sweet.

In hip hop, nobody said it like Big Daddy Kane,
Respect yourself and others, stay in your own lane.
I take my own advice, no hypocrite here,
Just striving every day to live sincere.

This isn't aimed at anyone – just sharing a truth,
Blessed with knowledge since my early youth.
No college required to see what's clear,
Wisdom comes from living without doubt or fear.

No matter where you're from or who you reppin,
If you don't like it, too bad, get to **steppin.**

Love, Relationships & Trust

Love can be beautiful, but it's not always easy. These poems
speak of the joy, the heartbreak, and the lessons I've learned
about trust and respect.

Inspired by Tevin Campbell

"Can We Talk"

This poem takes its name from a timeless 1993 song,
A tune that stays with us, cherished for so long.
The lyrics are smooth, romantic, and true,
I relate to them – they ease my mind too.

Talking brings us closer, helps friendships grow,
It lets us learn and share what we know.
With mutual respect and kindness in sight,
We create bonds that feel just right.

Can we talk? I already know your name,
The way you treat me, I'll treat you the same.

Won't give up easily but never force or stalk.
Standing here with thoughts ready to spark,
Hoping to connect – **can we talk.**

Inspired by The S.O.S. Band

"Just Be Good"

This classic hit, "Just Be Good to Me" by the S.O.S. Band,
A timeless track that'll make you hold your partner's hand.
Family and friends know I've got skills with rhyme,
I always give my best – it's my moment to shine.

I never thought I'd fall in love or take the chance,
But it happened unexpectedly with that first glance.
To everyone out there, this message is clear:
Do right, show respect, and stay away from fear.

I had enough, won't tolerate the same,
So please, no taking advantage – it's time to refrain.
Thank you to the real ones who genuinely care,
Appreciation matters, so let's all try to share.

It's sad some relationships lack what's a must,
Love, respect, honesty, and faith that's just.
Instead, jealousy and betrayal leave hearts in the dust,
When truth and devotion are all we can trust.

As I close this poem, I hold onto hope for the good,
Keep the faith, stay strong, and believe as you should.
Prayers up for blessings and peace understood,
Remember to always, **just be good!**

Inspired by Shalamar

"Second Chances"

There are many experiences we have once, twice,
And through them, we gain wisdom and advice.
No matter who, what, or where it may be,
Patience is key – so try, you'll see.

Jobs, friendships, relationships – they're like a game,
Circumstances shift, and no two are the same.
If the opportunity's worth it, people take their chances,
Hoping for growth and better advances.

This world holds events hard to explain,
When bad things happen, they leave a stain.
Yet when troubles strike, most sympathize,
Sharing pain through caring eyes.

Life is full of choices, we choose our way,
With hopes to succeed and brighten each day.
If God forgives, then so will I,
But don't assume that chances never run dry.

Some acts leave wounds that time enhances,
But remember, there won't always be **second chances.**

"Trippin"

In 1998, the song "Trippin" was made,
By talented ladies – Kima, Keisha, and Pam who slayed.
A classic so timeless, every time it would play,
People would smile and say, "That's my jam today!"

Too many have been played – fooled without a clue,
It's just another lesson learned – no more, no less, it's true.
No, I'm not speaking on anyone's case,
But be real – say what you want, like Total and Mase.

Be strong, be smart, and treat others with care,
Bring peace to the world – it's needed everywhere.
We need less drama, less pain, less buggin,
One of the reasons why people keep thuggin.

Betrayal, bad attitudes, and cheating bring strife,
They make people stumble, it's an unsettling life.
That's why it's best to do right and keep from slippin,
Please chill with the nonsense and stop **trippin.**

Inspired by Young Gunz

"Better Love"

Does anyone truly understand its definition?
From what I've seen, the way some act gives no recognition.
Many times, I've been guarded and stayed reserved,
Unsure if the love I witnessed was what I deserved.

I've felt uneasy, mistakes turning smiles to frowns,
Questioning if love is more than just ups and downs.
I believed it should embody honesty, loyalty, and trust,
A deep care shared between hearts – that's a must.

In the past, I admit I didn't know love's true feeling,
Relationships left me unsure, hearts not revealing.
But lessons learned have guided my resolve,
No empty words will pull me in or evolve.

I try not to let negativity cloud my view,
Reflecting deeply on what love means, staying true.
If love should come again, I'll tread with care,
Keeping my guard, yet striving to be fair.

Through it all, my faith in the Almighty prevails,
The belief that His guidance never fails.
And one thing I know that I truly deserve,
Is a love that's sincere, a love with no reserve.
What I seek now is something to rise above,
A bond that's pure – it's **better love.**

Inspired by Roberta Flack and Donny Hathaway

"The Closer I'll Get To"

The path ahead may seem distant and wide,
But with faith and strength, hope will always guide.
At times, space is what we need to grow,
A chance to reflect, to let our hearts show.

Sometimes distance provides a clearer view,
Where small acts of kindness feel sincere and true.
Roberta Flack and Donny Hathaway's song,
Showed how love's legacy remains so long.

Since 1978, their song has played,
A melody of love that will never fade.
It teaches us to cherish what's good and right,
And to embrace what brings our hearts delight.

No matter the trials or what we go through,
If you're close to me, **the closer I'll get to.**

Inspired by Mary J. Blige

"Love Without A Limit"

True love flows freely, with no bounds in sight,
It's felt from the heart, bringing warmth and light.
Actions speak louder than words we declare,
Genuine love is shown through how much we care.

A kind and sincere soul carries love's grace,
Respectful deeds leave a lasting trace.
Mary J. Blige's tune, a Hip-Hop Queen's decree,
Captures the essence of love for all to see.

Love is boundless, it needs no frame,
It grows and thrives without a name.
Through every moment, it brightly glows,
A force eternal, wherever it goes.

Let this be my vow, my heart's true exhibit,
I give my all, with **love without a limit.**

Inspired by Dru Hill

"Make A Promise"

A promise is a vow that's meant to be true,
Only to be made when it's clear what you'll do.
It's not just a word, but a pact that runs deep,
To be thoughtful and sincere in the ones you keep.

Never make a promise resonates deep and true,
Dru Hill reminds us to cherish what we do.
Though commitments may weaken, their value survives,
They shape our journey and the essence of our lives.

For me, a promise is a bond I'll defend,
My word holds true until the very end.
So if you choose to give your word, use care and be honest,
It matters the most when you **make a promise.**

Inspired by Keyshia Cole and Monica

"Trust"

Trust can be fragile when wrongs are done,
Without reason or cause, leaving faith to run.
Yet offering a chance without fear or delay,
Shows the strength to believe in kindness today.

I've always felt that if God forgives, so can I,
Faith and hope keep me uplifted, standing high.
Being taken for granted brings a sense of relief,
When holding fast to hope and unshaken belief.

Cheating's one of the worst acts, it's said time and again,
So I raise my guard, careful with whom I befriend.
Friendships, family, and bonds of any kind,
Place belief as a cornerstone, strong and defined.

It's so important I've inked it on my wrist,
A constant reminder that trust must persist.
Forgetting may not come, but forgiveness should be a must,
With honesty and loyalty, we strengthen our **trust.**

Inspired by Raphael Saadiq and Tony! Toni! Tone!

"That's All I Ask"

Some requests we make shouldn't always feel grand,
It depends on the moment, but be real, take a stand.
Life's not as simple as we'd hope or desire,
There are hurdles to face and challenges to inspire.

Disagreements arise, yet less may be more,
Hard work earns its value, a truth we can't ignore.
Lessons are learned, even when hope falls flat,
Growth from the struggles is where wisdom is at.

"That's All I Ask of You," as Tony! Toni! Tone! once sang,
It's a melody of meaning, where truths often hang.
Regardless of the answer, yes or no, I'll stay composed,
In my own space, where calmness is enclosed.

All we need could make life's burdens feel bright,
I'm thankful for much but won't waste time in spite.
Treat my moments with care, a simple, fair task,
I'll keep it quite clear – **that's all I ask.**

"Karma"

The word karma carries weight and meaning strong,
It shapes our paths as we journey along.
The title of songs by both Banks and Keys –
It's life's realities, not for birds or bees.

I don't wish harm, not even on my foes;
For those I love, it's a truth that shows.
So many bad things – wrong and outrageous,
Unacceptable acts, cruel and contagious.

What goes around comes back around –
A lesson most have seen, heard, or found.
In life's uncertain turns, the choice is clear;
Kindness beats being mean, year after year.

We meet people everywhere – from streets to the sky,
But heartbreak's the worst when betrayal's nearby.
Being cheated on leaves wounds too heavy to bear,
Yet selfishness drives some to be unfair.

It takes strength to endure and rise above pain,
To face every trial and still remain sane.
Walk with respect; let kindness be your armor,
For life always circles back – that's called **karma**.

Inspired by Jodeci

"Lady"

It doesn't matter if you're a woman or man,
We all have feelings, minds, and our own plan.
I truly admire those who are honest and kind –
Trustworthy and respectful, with a noble mind.

In a world so wide with billions near and far,
Life keeps evolving – new lessons shape who we are.
I've learned to be cautious, observant, and wise,
After facing the nonsense, games, and lies.

A genuine soul, I love to create,
To write, chill, and enjoy music that's great.
With faith, joy, and strength, my smile shines through –
Living life fully, as I know I'm meant to do.

I might not fit the mold some may define,
But my style and confidence are uniquely mine.
With a heart so big, though once broken apart,
It's mended by faith and a resilient heart.

From now on, people get the respect they bring;
The energy they give is the tune I'll sing.
No angel or saint – but trust, I'm not shady;
I'm just a smart, loving, loyal, beautiful **lady**.

Hardship, Healing & Strength

Whether it's personal pain or what's happening in the world, these poems speak on real struggles – and the strength it takes to keep going when times get tough.

Inspired by The Stop the Violence Movement

"Stop The Violence"

Racism in this world is one of the worst,
What truly matters should always come first.
Billions of people, diverse in culture and race,
Hatred divides us, leaving a bitter trace.

I'd rather be thankful, to witness the sun,
Than see harm done with words or a gun.
Judging by color is cruel and unkind,
Respect for each other brings peace of mind.

Killings and violence tear lives apart,
Fueling pain that weighs heavy on the heart.
Some who wear blue don't fulfill their role,
While others serve proudly with heart and soul.

We must face the truth and stand to unite,
For love is the answer to make things right.
Life's greatest lessons, they teach us to be strong,
Hatred and racism have lasted too long.

Let's lift up our voices, breaking through the silence,
And loudly declare: **Stop the Violence.**

Inspired by Monie Love

"It's A Shame"

This song is a true, classic throwback,
A gem from a 1991 track.
The dawn of an era, when hip-hop was pure,
Full of fun – its energy felt secure.

True Image said – he messed around with her heart,
A feeling too real, but unknown at the start.
I don't know if you agree, but I truly feel –
When she said – the way he hurt me, it was so real.

Too many have been taken for granted and used,
Good men and women left broken, abused.
No relationship should endure an aggressor or victim,
That chaos leads only to a broken system.

Each day brings thoughts – every minute, every hour,
Our journeys are rooted in strength and power.
The lesson is clear – stay away from the game,
Monie Love said it best – **it's a shame.**

Inspired by Musiq Soulchild

"Crazy"

It's clear to many how chaos and crime prevail,
Coupled with the fleeting pace of time we all trail.

Some find themselves overwhelmed by the world's pace,
Seeking refuge in peace, a safe and quiet space.
In the turmoil, we cling to the small comforts that heal,
Finding serenity in relaxed moments where time feels real.

Life can get so crazy, some lose their peace of mind,
Exploding in anger that's hard to unwind.

Mentally, physically, or emotionally – stay aware,
Guard yourself from dangers that lurk everywhere.
Drama spreads swiftly, and betrayal's just a waste,
I'll always choose peace over an unwelcome space.

Having more or better doesn't make others lazy,
Kindness is key, so don't tempt me to become **crazy.**

Inspired by the Geto Boys

"The Mind Playing Tricks"

The mind played tricks on Scarface, Willie D, and Bill,
Together they crafted a song full of skill.
There have been moments when I felt unsure,
But no manipulation – I've kept my thoughts pure.

I didn't know Scarface repped the Geto Boys' name,
Writing these poems, I've earned some fame.
Yes, my mind has tricked me once or twice,
But staying calm and grounded feels so nice.

Bushwick Bill, may you rest in peace,
Your work and impact will never cease.
You even shined on 'Martin,' a classic show,
A memory cherished by fans who know.

Some minds stand firm, like solid bricks,
But stay alert – beware of **the mind playing tricks.**

Inspired by Mary J. Blige

"Worry"

There are times in life when challenges take shape,
From family to health, or work we can't escape.
It's a feeling we all know, and though it may linger,
Strength and resilience often rest in our fingers.

Concerns can weigh heavy, like clouds in the sky,
But kindness and faith are the reasons we try.
Even when storms come and uncertainty presses,
We find ways to embrace life's small successes.

Life is rarely simple, stress often takes hold,
But blessings still shine, as life's stories unfold.
Though time moves quickly, there's no need to hurry,
So I promise myself not to always **worry.**

Inspired by Angie Stone

"No More Rain"

The clouds have cleared, and my sunshine is here to stay,
With love, I radiate joy and warmth in every possible way.
The beam of the sun and sky lifts spirits when it's bright,
Just as the stars and the moon bring magic to the night.

A heartfelt tribute to Angie Stone, may she rest in peace.
Music, filled with soul, carries a tone that will never cease.
Her melodies echo with a beauty that's tender and true,
Leaving a lasting impression in all that they pursue.

Raindrops falling from the sky, like teardrops of sorrow,
Reflecting the burden of struggles and hope for tomorrow.
But as the storm subsides and the sun rises once again,
Despair fades – light returns in many women and men.

The vision is clear – a life filled with joy and a little refrain,
From the weight of storm clouds, and from **no more rain.**

Inspired by Smokey Robinson

"The Track Of My Tears"

"The Track of My Tears" takes us on a journey far back,
Smokey Robinson and the Miracles – a legendary track.
Behind the smile, emotions slowly unfold,
Revealing a story too heavy to be told.

Each tear that falls leaves a visible line,
A trail of feelings, both deep and divine.
When the smile returns, the tears will cease,
Marking a rise of inner peace.

Support and love bring healing through the years,
Easing the sorrow and calming the fears.
Timeless music offers comfort and grace,
A haven of solace in life's vast space.

I'm forever thankful for melodies that appear,
For nothing heals quite like **"The Track of My Tears."**

Inspired by DMX and Faith Evans

"I Really Miss You"

Nearly every day, I find myself in thought,
Of loved ones lost and the love they brought.
The weight of grief is more than words can show,
A burden I carry wherever I go.

I'll never forget my aunts, uncles, cousins, and Shane,
Missing the moments we'll never regain.
Not being able to hug or talk feels surreal,
The absence cuts deeper than words reveal.

Both of my grandmothers, gentle and sweet,
Their love and care made life complete.
I know they've found peace, which eases the strain,
But I wish they weren't forever in that domain.

This message is for my little ones and loved ones I adore,
They will always be in my heart, now and evermore.
From the very beginning, my love has stayed,
Unwavering, unchanging, never delayed.

We've all lost someone we hold so dear,
And although they're gone, their spirits are near.
RIP to both my grandmothers and other family too,
Forever in my heart – **I really miss you.**

Positivity, Growth & Motivation

Even on the hard days, I choose to keep going. These poems are about staying focused, keeping faith, and finding peace in the process.

Inspired by the Five Stairsteps

"Oooh Child"

Oooh Child, things will get brighter – the words say,
A powerful reminder to keep striving every day.
Through challenges and trials, I stand even higher,
With hope in my heart, my dreams won't expire.

Whenever I hear Oooh Child, my mind drifts back,
To Boyz n the Hood, where its positivity made an impact.
That iconic scene remains such a heartfelt delight,
Adding depth to a moment filled with hope and light.

I may not know everything about the Five Stairsteps' art,
But their song has always held a special place in my heart.
It's a tune I grew up cherishing, and it's still a treasure –
Timeless and uplifting, it delivers joy without measure.

In a world where so much can feel wild and out of place,
I think of how time flies as children grow with grace.
Reflecting on the journey, with emotions running wild,
The only response is to say, **Oooh Child.**

Inspired by Tyrese

"Stay"

In life, we face the choice to stay or part,
Each decision is ours, though it may weigh on the heart.
It's up to us, despite who might protest,
Our path is ours to follow, and to live our best.

I've learned not to lower my standards or feel shame,
Even when hardship strikes or I'm met with blame.
Some moments were not meant to unfold as they did,
But growth and wisdom emerge, so lessons aren't hid.

If I'm ever unwelcome or pushed aside,
I'll rise with resilience and stand with pride.
Rejection is something we all endure,
Yet I stand firm, grounded, and pure.

Respect to those who admit when they're wrong,
Acknowledgment and growth make us strong.
Whether in love or life, we find our way,
But one truth remains – it's not always easy to **stay.**

Inspired by LL Cool J

"Better"

I seek good advice and fresh ideas with care,
Though I don't always show it, the feeling is still there.
I strive to stay optimistic, no matter the trials I face,
Even in pain or sorrow, I hold on to grace.

Through times of hardship, anything bad or tragic,
I cling onto faith, still believing in magic.
It's what many of us carry when life first begin,
Adapting each day, keeping hope deep within.

Each step forward is a lesson, each setback a chance,
To realign our purpose and rethink our stance.
Life isn't perfect, but it's a journey we must embrace,
Finding joy in the moments and strength in the race.

This poem is my way to share how I feel,
No letter this time, but the message is real.
To everyone I know and love, no matter the weather,
I hold onto hope that things will get **better.**

Inspired by Deniece Williams

"Miracle"

Each miracle feels special, a blessing so rare,
Bringing joy and tears that show how we care.
Someday, I hope one big miracle appears,
Enough to calm my worries and quiet my fears.

My faith is strong, though I've been stuck before,
Still, wishing others luck opens a brighter door.
Miracles don't arrive at a planned or hoped time,
They follow their own rhythm, their own unique rhyme.

Still, love must grow, and hate must fade,
So much in this world needs kindness displayed.
Let's keep faith alive and hearts strong and pure,
For blessings, better health, and bonds that endure.

To me, life's sweetest gift would truly be,
Becoming a mom again and thriving happily.
Like melodies of love, both rich and lyrical,
Tomorrow's light may reveal a **miracle.**

"Let Go"

Certain people and memories still cross the mind,
Though rare, a truly special connection is hard to find.
Mike Shorey and Fabolous once expressed in their song,
Holding on tight, even when it's wrong.

But promises faded, chasing the thrill,
Love should uplift, yet it lingers still.
Letting go isn't easy, but reclaiming space,
Brings peace and freedom at one's own pace.

Maybe staying single is the better call,
Because heartbreak and betrayal aren't worth it at all.
Self-love matters – stay aware and alert,
Cherish your worth; don't settle for hurt.

Some only rebound – but why play that game,
Never be an option or wait in vain.
Some things aren't forever, as Lil' Mo let us know,
And when love isn't valued, it's time to **let go.**

"Joy Over Pain"

Many have faced struggles and endured some pain,
Yet everyone seeks joy, like sunshine after rain.
Life tests us all, whether girl or boy,
But it also gives us moments of pure, radiant joy.

Smiles, laughter, and news worth celebrating,
Lift our spirits to a place that's elevating.
Frankie Beverly & Maze's "Joy and Pain",
A timeless classic that will always remain.

Through melodies that heal and lyrics that soar,
Music reminds us what life is worth fighting for.
In every note, we find courage to stand,
A universal power that unites and command.

Hard as stone, pain can weigh us down,
But joy lifts us up, erasing the frown.
I'll take the sunshine, and less of the rain,
And most would agree – choose **joy over pain.**

Inspired by Scarface, Tupac and Lloyd Banks

"Smile"

Inspired by Scarface, Tupac, and Lloyd Banks,
Two iconic songs that led me to write this poem, so thanks.
It's always a joy to see people laugh and smile,
A moment of peace that can last a while.

Wouldn't it be wonderful to see it in all,
Women, girls, men, and boys – big or small.
Some show their smiles, whether kind or not,
If blessed with life, smile, even when it's all you've got.

When someone's upset, you'll notice their bad side,
So to prevent it, don't piss them off, just let it slide

I've been through a lot, both present and past,
Still I smile, not knowing which moment could be my last.

Some feel trapped, wanting to be free,
But brighter days will come – just wait, you'll see.
Cherish the good times, let joy compile,
Laughter is healing – so go on and **smile.**

Inspired by Luther Vandross

"So Amazing"

Happiness, joy, and moments of cheer,
Good news and laughter that bring us near.
The warmth of a smile, as bright as the sun,
Fills life with blessings and makes it fun.

Every day I'm grateful for this life I lead,
Through ups and downs, I find what I need.
I focus on positivity and keeping the peace,
Finding calm in writing, my soul's release.

Family time, holidays, and moments we share,
Remind me of the love and joy we declare.
Life holds treasures for those who embrace,
The beauty of moments and life's gentle grace.

Here's to success, bright futures, and more,
To memories that uplift and deeply restore.
With love, prayers, and joy always blazing,
Life's precious moments are just **so amazing.**

Inspired by Ice Cube

"A Good Day"

Every day starts with heartfelt appreciation,
Giving thanks to God for endless inspiration.
Many hope for good days, simple and bright,
Instead of odd ones that don't feel right.

No matter the day, I strive to feel blessed,
Even when challenges put me to the test.
Today was good, I echo with pride,
Just like Ice Cube, with joy as my guide.

Grateful for the love that comes my way,
From Facebook and TikTok, it brightens my day.
Life's full of ups and downs, this is true,
But staying authentic is what I always pursue.

So here's my wish as I pass this your way,
Stay safe, stay strong, and have **a good day.**

Inspired by Lionel Richie

"Easy"

Life feels simple, with no stress in the air,
Surrounded by love, true bonds we declare.
Set a trend of kindness, let joy take the lead,
Spreading understanding is all that we need.

Stories and legacies wait to be explored,
In quiet reflection, their meanings restored.
Though challenges may come, and trials may rise,
Embrace them with calm – see life through clear eyes.

Heritage and love may test us, it's true,
Yet patience and peace reveal a brighter view.
Lessons are constant, their impact stays breezy,
So in all that you do, remember to stay **easy.**

Inspired by Patrice Rushen

"Feels So Real"

When it feels so real, my mind won't let go,
A choice that's mine, no matter what others show.
Honesty shines where disguises fade,
No surprise when truths are honestly displayed.

Patrice Rushen's song from back in '84,
A timeless melody that I adore.
Promises forgotten leave hearts in pain,
Yet deep feelings remain like sunshine in rain.

Each step I take is guided by the light,
Positivity leads through the darkest night.
Mistakes are chances to learn and correct,
With truth paving paths of love and respect.

Life will challenge, but love's warmth can heal,
Nothing compares to when it **feels so real.**

"Put A Little Rush"

Sometimes in life, a little rush can play its part,
Pushing us forward, igniting the spark in our heart.
Moments of urgency, when success is the prize,
Make the effort worthwhile, as dreams start to rise.

"You're Puttin a Rush on Me," by Stephanie is a classic,
Its message of grace and balance is fantastic.
While some tasks require speed, like paying those bills,
Other things, like relationships, needs patience and thrills.

Stephanie's intention was clear with a thoughtful tone,
Taking her time, letting emotions flourish and be shown.
Falling in love isn't easy when emotions collide,
But she shows how to move with care and pride.

Emotions run wild when it starts as a crush,
Yet love always knows when to **put a little rush.**

Inspired by The Isley Brothers

"Don't Change"

No need to change, unless it's for the best,
I meant every word, no need to second-guess.
Through all the negativity, one thought remains,
This lesson stays constant in my heart and brain.

Changes may come, both good and bad,
Life has its highs and lows that make us glad or sad.

Take strength in the love that others may bring,
It's the bond between hearts that makes life sing.
Through thick and thin, hold onto what's true,
And let kindness and compassion guide you through.

Wishing you the best in all that you pursue,
Sending love and prayers – please send some too.
It's a shame some things in life feel so strange,
To all the kind souls out there, please **don't change.**

Inspired by R. Kelly and The Notorious B.I.G.

"Be Happy"

Day and night, he lifts his hopes high,
That love will return – it won't pass him by.
R. Kelly and Biggie spoke words so true,
But being happy is a gift, yet it can fade too.

Despite the struggles, happiness deserves to stay,
To light up our lives in a beautiful way.
We all deserve to feel how we choose,
Just be genuine, there's nothing to lose.

I rather chill, stay calm, and not get snappy,
Hoping that most people will try to **be happy**.

Music, Rhythm & Artistic Inspiration

Music raised me, healed me, and inspired my writing. These poems are tributes to some of the artists who helped shape my style and my soul.

Inspired by Michael Jackson

"Rock With You"

On August 29, 1958, a star was born,
Michael Jackson's style redefined the norm.
His iconic white glove and moves so refined,
Forever etched in the hearts of humankind.

His music is timeless – a rhythm so real,
A soft-spoken voice but a presence to feel.
With spins and glides, his steps always amaze,
The moonwalk – an art deserving of praise.

In a family of talent, he stood out true,
A legend whose hits are more than a few.
"Rock with You" is a song I keep close,
A timeless masterpiece cherished the most.

RIP to a legend – his impact shines through,
Michael Jackson, forever inspires us to **rock with you.**

Inspired by The Isley Brothers

"Groove"

Another chance arises for a positive style,
Laid-back and cool, it's worth a smile.
Moments to jam and ease my heart,
Keeping calm is where I'll do my part.

Who doesn't love a great mood to share,
Music, romance, moments rare.
Relax, enjoy, and let good vibes flow,
Chill and groove where the feelings glow.

Time speeds by, but memories I'll hold,
Cherish the moments, whether quiet or bold.
Always for love, peace, and happiness, I strive,
Soaking up the beauty of life's vibrant vibe.

At the end of the day, what's left to prove,
Show more action, less words, and let's just **groove.**

Inspired by Snoop Dogg

"Snoop"

Countless tributes and verses that last,
Snoop Dogg's influence, both present and past.
A legend of rap, with style and finesse,
With wealth and hits, yet he avoids excess.

From "Gin and Juice" to unforgettable flows,
His catalog of classics continually grows.
Admired for his charisma and cool demeanor,
Snoop's legacy only becomes sharper and keener.

A West Coast king at the top of the scene,
Decades in, his skills remain supreme.
A family man with humor and charm,
Every step he takes leaves behind no harm.

His greatness shines through his timeless groove,
In Hip Hop and Rap, no one can remove.
With his legacy strong and always in the loop,
Forever celebrated, the one and only – **Snoop.**

Inspired by Ja Rule, Ashanti, Vita, and Charli Baltimore

"Down"

"Down for You," by Vita, Charli B., and Ja Rule,
A track so fire – it's timeless and cool.
Beats and lyrics hit deep, never sounding old,
A classic that's fresh, solid and bold.

Beyond Ashanti, how many strive to be that chic,
To hold it all down, not play games or be slick.
Choices are plenty – the mind steers the way,
What's wanted and desired shapes each day.

Staying focused, keeping my vision clear,
Driven by purpose, no room for fear.
Monica once spoke about emotions that can't be denied,
So embracing them fully, never pushing aside.

Obligations or not, life's choices still astound,
So much to determine, endless paths that surround.
Forever down for poetry, where creativity flows,
With no shame in the game, as gratitude grows.

Not everyone wears a crown, yet greatness stands tall,
With faith and respect, we rise through it all.
In a world that's searching for strength to be found,
Ask yourself truly – who is **down.**

Inspired by Erykah Badu

"Next Lifetime"

In this lifetime, there's so much to explore,
Moments of joy and blessings galore.
Erykah Badu's song speaks to the heart,
Her tale of another life, a timeless work of art.

Life unfolds in the choices we make,
From dreams we chase to steps we take.
Each moment shapes us, crafting our design,
Creating a journey uniquely mine.

Though questions arise as we climb uphill,
Hope and faith uplift our spirits still.
Love remains constant, a radiant sign,
Promising connection through space and time.

No matter the hurdles or mountains we climb,
It would be beautiful to meet in the **next lifetime.**

Inspired by Aaliyah

"Back & Forth"

Who else moves forward yet forgives and looks back?
I hope for a brighter future, while cutting some slack.
Back and Forth, isn't always a fight or debate –
It holds deeper meaning, which some may relate.

Aaliyah's music was a bridge between past and present,
Her style and rhythm were uniquely vibrant and pleasant.
"Back and Forth" teaches us to embrace life's pace,
To honor the moments that time can't erase.

Each lyric, each beat, resonates with meaning,
Reminding us that life's balance is intervening.
Aaliyah, our beloved Baby Girl, sang with such groove,
Her voice carried rhythm that made the world move.

A throwback hit from 1994, cherished in every place –
Still celebrated worldwide with love and grace.
This poem's for Aaliyah – her talent shined from the North;
With one of her best legendary songs – **"Back & Forth."**

Inspired by Aretha Franklin

"A Beautiful Rose"

Roses are red, violets are blue,
They're pretty and sweet – that much is true.
They bloom in colors, big and small,
One of the best flowers of all.

Getting flowers makes my heart shine,
A loving gift that feels so divine.
A rose is still a rose – I love it, Aretha sang with soul,
She had inspiration, and people knew her goal.

Whenever someone brings flowers my way,
I accept them, and they brighten my day.
They may not last, their petals may close,
But I'll always remember **a beautiful rose.**

Inspired by Eric B. & Rakim

"Soul"

A soul resides within us all, good or bad,
Many bring joy and kindness, while others turn sad.
Some souls may wander, lost and unseen,
But I vow to keep mine pure and clean.

Finding peace and manifesting is key,
Faith and prayer, yes, they inspire me.
The soul isn't just outside, but deep inside,
An essence the beholder cannot hide.

I celebrate being a woman of strength and pride,
Always here to offer help and be a guide.
So much soul lives in music's embrace,
From RnB, Rap, and Hip Hop's grace.

Each day I'm thankful for talent and life's role,
And hope to meet others with hearts so whole.
Through music and passion, we lift and console,
Connected forever by rhythm and **soul.**

Self-Reflection & Life Lessons

Growth isn't always pretty, but it's real. These poems are me checking myself, learning, and growing wiser.

Inspired by Nice & Smooth

"I Rhyme Slow"

I take my time, making sure each word flows,
Creating poetry that speaks and shows.
Inspired by Nice and Smooth's perfect track,
At times I rhyme slow, keeps me coming back.

Writing gives me peace and lifts my soul,
Every line feels like it makes me whole.
When my poems are done, I smile and share,
Blowing a kiss into the open air.

My style remains steady, thoughtful and strong,
Every poem reflects the values I've held all along.
If the rhythm fades, it's plain to see,
The missing rhyme wouldn't belong to me.

Some craft their lines with a rapid-fire pace,
But I embrace a rhythm that lets me find grace.
This is where I shine; my style, my glow,
It's who I am, and that's why **I rhyme slow.**

Inspired by The Whispers

"Say Yes"

How often do we wish to hear yes instead of no,
In debates or struggles, some just accept and let it go.
Honestly, I don't like being left out or turned away,
From good things in life that brighten the day.

Maybe if I were treated the same way I desire,
I'd say yes more often – it's a goal to aspire.
Life's lessons remind us, like Earth, Wind & Fire,
Respect, love, and prosperity are virtues to admire.

We learn through the years that things don't always align,
Though feelings may sway, we respect voices over time.
There are moments I've wanted but would never impose,
And through wisdom gained, I let life's path compose.

Every decision doesn't have to cause distress,
Life unfolds in ways we can't always guess.
Sometimes, the simple choice is to just **say yes.**

Inspired by Alicia Myers

"The Best From Me"

Are there good-hearted souls who hope for the best,
Who don't act superior or above the rest.
Yes, they exist, and they shine so bright,
Spreading love and kindness, a guiding light.

A soul so bright and a heart full of grace,
Outshining titles in every space.
Aretha Franklin made it clear in her song,
Respect is a value that keeps us strong.

Working hard, with faith to believe,
Pushing for goals we aim to achieve.
Yet compassion, courage, and treating others right,
Are what this world needs to reignite.

So, keep moving forward, and give to those you see,
Lift others around you with hope and glee.
Like Alicia Myers sang with such harmony,
I'll always strive to give **the best from me.**

Inspired by Kelly Price

"Should Have Told Me"

When someone has something to say, speak your mind,
Don't always hold back – don't stay confined.
It's no problem for me, I'll stay on track,
Nothing personal, but I used to react.

I would get offended, unless it was right,
Then I'd be defensive, ready to fight.
He should have told her, I'm talking about Kelly Price,
She made it clear, and her song was nice.

Not all secrets should get tucked away,
No matter how tough, some truths must stay.
So much won't be tolerated – enough is enough,
Can't keep accepting the same old stuff.

People will always go where they need to be,
By choice or obligation – but still, **should have told me.**

Inspired by Keith Sweat

"Twisted"

Some people seem to have it twisted,
Pretending they know it all.
But empty words mean nothing,
When actions fail to stand tall.

Respect and kindness should guide the way,
Lifting others up every single day.
It takes strength to choose what's right,
And keep your integrity shining bright.

A foundation of goodwill should anchor each bond,
Helping us rise and move beyond.
Standing for what's right takes courage within –
Integrity glows through the thick and thin.

Two songs have "Twisted" in their name,
Keith Sweat's version isn't the same.
Though my thoughts aren't all listed,
Every story has two sides – so don't get it **twisted.**

Inspired by Anita Baker

"Apology"

Has everyone ever truly said they're sorry aloud.
For mistakes they've made or actions they're not proud.
I've said it myself, many times before,
Even when anger knocked at my door.

Some strive so hard just to do what's right,
Because peace of mind helps you sleep through the night.
Whether others agree or choose to rebel,
Life is full of stories that I could tell – and maybe sell.

I often wonder why kind hearts endure so much,
Life twists and turns – some things we shouldn't touch.
Struggles are plenty, but the goal is to thrive,
And always be thankful to simply be alive.

Pleasure P's, "Did You Wrong" speaks to the pain,
I've felt it deeply, but it won't remain.
I'll stay collected and let my grace be my stride,
You crossed that line once, but I won't let it slide.

Havoc and Prodigy noted, it's all twisted, it's true,
But sincerity matters in all that we do.
Mistakes may happen, that's part of life's astrology,
But maturity shows when you offer an honest **apology.**

Inspired by Christopher Williams

"Dream"

A dream drifts deep, where memories hold tight,
Reflections of New Jack City still shine bright.
A soundtrack that shaped a moment in time,
A classic that lingers, with rhythm divine.

Dreams come in forms – the good and the bad,
But my favorite ones bring memories that I've had.
Of my loved ones gone, their faces I see,
The sweetest dreams that mean the most to me.

Have you ever had a nightmare so real,
It shook your spirit with fear you could feel.
I've had my share, they gave me a fright,
Waking suddenly in the dead of night.

Belief in God, angels, and heaven is strong,
It's a faith I've carried all my life long.
Dreams and premonitions, peaceful and bright,
So vivid, they make you hold them tight.

Some bring comfort, others bring fear,
Some feel so close, like they're drawing near.
And although nightmares may seem extreme,
You wake up and realize – it was only just a **dream.**

Inspired by Lyfe Jennings

"Must Be Nice"

To receive kindness, give it in return,
Those who do wrong will one day learn.
And if not, at least be fair,
Consider others in times of despair.

Life's too short to carry hate,
Lifting others makes us great.
Been nice all my life, so there's nothing to doubt,
Trust and believe – many could point it out.

Karma is real, it has been said more than twice,
Every action comes with some kind of price.
Some walk in peace, others roll the dice,
Lyfe Jennings made it clear – **must be nice.**

Inspired by Yolanda Adams

"Open Up My Heart"

Yolanda Adams shares her heart with grace,
A soul and voice that time won't erase.
Her words inspire, a message so strong,
Giving with love should never feel wrong.

A heart once open, now weathered and torn,
Shaped by trials, by lessons worn.
Still faith remains, through highs and lows,
Finding wisdom as each season flows.

This heart lifts first to God above,
Then to those deserving of love.
Amazing Grace still moves the soul,
But time reveals who to hold.

If the past could change and wrongs undo,
Each wound would heal, the soul renew.
Yet scars remain where lessons start,
Still, I rise to **open up my heart.**

Inspired by Beanie Sigel

"In The Air"

Something feels off, a shift in the air,
A warning sensed but hard to declare.
Beanie Sigel captured that vibe so well,
A feeling too deep for words to tell.

Nothing beats the freshness of a breeze,
The kind that makes flowers bloom with ease.
A crisp wind that carries no sting,
Just pure calm as the seasons sing.

Some voices linger, their meaning so clear,
A rhythm felt when the message draws near.
Do you feel it too – that unspoken sound,
A melody that echoes all around.

And when rain falls, some pull away,
Storms can turn peace into dismay.
Not everyone loves lightning's spark,
Or thunder rumbling deep in the dark.

Winter arrives, cold yet bright,
Bringing warmth in festive light.
Agree or not, just pause and stare,
And wonder what else drifts **in the air.**

Inspired by Midnight Star

"Curious"

Curiosity sparks when the mind feels free,
Unlocking the doors to all it can see.
Thoughts take shape as new wonders appear,
Seeking the truths that feel bright and clear.

Midnight Star's rhythm, smooth and true,
Moves with a groove that carries us through.
Curiosity stirs the dreams we chase,
Guiding each step, time, and place.

Some search for wisdom, some only pry,
One seeks to learn, the other asks why.
A restless mind won't settle or stray,
It longs for knowledge in its own way.

Through every lesson, through each test,
Wisdom grows and stands the quest.
No matter the path, the drive is mysterious,
Forever seeking – always **curious.**

Inspired by SWV

"Right Here"

I always hoping that my family and friends stay safe,
Wishing them peace, love, and blessings in their space.
Daily prayers feel natural, but at night they're profound,
Reflecting on life's meaning and the joys we've found.

It warms my heart to be in the presence of those I love,
These connections are a treasure, a gift from above.
Nobody wants to feel neglected or treated with fear,
So I've learned to spread love and keep them near.

Work hard to achieve, but embrace moments of rest,
Taking time when needed can truly be best.
Not everyone admits they care, but the love sincere,
If you think or worry about me, just know I'm **right here.**

"They Don't Know"

Proof is good to offer when someone's unsure;
There were times I assumed, but my heart remains pure.
Jon B's "They Don't Know" feels like it fits right,
Funny how jealousy hides until it steps into the light.

With hidden meanings layered deep in the sound,
It's the kind of song where true emotions are found.
Jon B's voice, a mix of passion and class,
Pulls you into a story that's destined to last.
The beats whisper secrets, and the lyrics do too,
It resonates with moments that feel so true.

Not sure exactly who he was singing about,
But one thing's for sure, his style leaves no doubt.
I won't deny – I like to talk, though action's what I show.
So until the truth is found, guess **they don't know.**

Legacy, Family & Bonds

The people I love – those still with me and those I've lost –
mean the world to me. These poems are about connections,
memories, and the kind of love that stays with you.

Inspired by Sister Sledge

"We Are Family And Friends"

Family and friends fill my life in countless ways,
Their love and laughter brighten my days.
I cherish those who've gone away,
While holding close the ones who stay.

Two grandmothers, strong and wise,
Guiding with love, through joyful highs.
Sister Sledge's song plays in my mind,
A melody where love and unity bind.

Though distance may keep some apart,
Respect and care live in my heart.
The memories of school still shine,
Where friendships formed and love aligned.

Linwood, North Brunswick & McKinley too,
Taught lessons in life – some tough, some true.
Through highs and lows, the love extends,
Forever united – **we are family and friends.**

Inspired by Glenn Jones

"Only Just Begun"

Each year opens a door to new beginnings,
With gratitude for life's countless winnings.
March 21st, a date I deeply hold dear,
Filled with love, joy, and laughter to cheer.

Blessing drift gently to the skies above,
With candles glowing and clovers of love.
Glenn Jones song, "We've Only Just Begun,"
A reminder that life's journey is never done.

Beginnings hold promises we should cherish,
Moments to nurture so they never perish.
Patience and time reveal life's design,
Every step forward makes the journey divine.

Embrace each day, let life's joy run,
And live it fully, like it's **only just begun.**

Inspired by Jagged Edge

"Good Luck Charm"

Luck is something we all need in life,
A little extra hope to handle the strife.
Even when focused or feeling stuck,
A charm reminds us to believe in our luck.

Beautiful and meaningful, charms hold their appeal,
Their magic doesn't always have to be real.
Wishing good fortune for the people we love,
Sending positivity from the stars above.

In a world that often feels heavy and gray,
Better things are needed to brighten the day.
Like "Good Luck Charm" by Jagged Edge, a tune divine,
A reminder of moments where hope will shine.

Appreciate the treasures we hold in our arms,
Jewelry or not, there's nothing like a **good luck charm.**

Inspired by Jaheim

"Just In Case"

Jaheim's voice carries wisdom and soul,
A reminder that life isn't always in our control.
While hoping for the best, we prepare for what may come,
Cherishing memories until time is done.

The past holds lessons, but the present leads the way,
Focusing on the future while honoring yesterday.
His music is timeless, a treasure to admire,
Celebrating life despite challenges that require.

Talented voices inspire emotion and grace,
Creating melodies that hold a special place.
From songs that touch to beats that ignite,
True artistry turns up the volume of delight.

Through every moment, love leaves a trace,
A reminder to live – **just in case.**

Inspired by The Game and Chris Brown

"Gold"

Silver or gold – which one shines bright,
Both bring joy when they feel just right.
"Pot of Gold" by The Game and Chris Brown,
A fitting tune for coins, trophies, or a crown.

Family and friends are treasures untold,
Their love outweighs the shimmer of gold.
Jewelry dazzles, a pleasure to find,
But true wealth comes from the heart and mind.

Many chase fortune, swayed by desire,
Placing possessions above what's higher.
It's easy to crave what seems well-earned,
Yet life's balance shifts as lessons are learned.

"Silver and Gold" by Shirley Caesar shines bright,
A gospel gem that shares wisdom and light.
Though we long for riches, bright and bold,
The greatest gifts aren't always **gold.**

"I Rhyme Every Time"

I write to express what's deep in my mind,
The words, the rhythm, they perfectly align.
Poetry is power, it's more than a rhyme,
It's who I am – **I rhyme every time.**

I rhyme through joy as well as pain,
Through sunshine bright or pouring rain.
Every verse, every line, every story is mine,
No matter what – **I rhyme every time.**

I rhyme for love, I rhyme for truth,
Through lessons learned and dreams of youth.
For voices unheard, for moments that shine,
And forever, always – **I rhyme every time.**

This Is Where It Ends